THE
PARABLES
of JESUS

D0881976

KENNETH SCHENCK

wesleyan
publishing
house

Indianapolis, Indiana

Copyright © 2013 by Kenneth Schenck
Published by Wesleyan Publishing House
Indianapolis, Indiana 46250
Printed in the United States of America
ISBN: 978-0-89827-738-8
ISBN (e-book): 978-0-89827-815-6

Library of Congress Cataloging-in-Publication Data

Schenck, Kenneth, 1966-
  The parables of Jesus / Kenneth Schenck.
     pages cm
  ISBN 978-0-89827-738-8
1. Jesus Christ--Parables--Devotional use. I. Title.
  BT375.3.S34 2013
  226.8'06--dc23

                        2013033137

CONTENTS

INTRODUCTION

The gospel of Mark says that Jesus taught the crowds "with many similar parables . . . as much as they could understand. He did not say anything to them without using a parable. But when he was alone with his own disciples, he explained everything" (4:33–34). Here we have the essence of Jesus' public teaching—he taught in short stories.

The parables take different forms in the Gospels. Some are very short comparisons, like the parable of the yeast: "The kingdom of heaven is like yeast that a woman took and mixed into about sixty pounds of flour until it worked all through the dough" (Matt. 13:33). Others are extended allegories, like the parable of the weeds, where different elements of the story all clearly stand for different things.

Some of the parables are more like riddles, meant to filter the audience in accordance with their faith (see Mark 4:11–12). The meaning of others seems fairly obvious, and Jesus' enemies knew he was talking about them (see Matt. 21:45–46). They remain some of the most memorable of Jesus' teachings, because the human brain is wired to remember stories, especially relatively brief ones.

This book presents six weeks of Bible studies on the parables of Jesus. Many of Jesus' parables made similar points, so it is not hard to group them according to similar themes. Week 1 looks at Jesus' parables having to do with seeds and weeds. The parable of the soils is, in a way, the key to all of Jesus' parables. But he also used other agricultural images to communicate powerfully to his agrarian, Galilean audiences.

Week 2 has parables about prodigals and the lost, which capture Jesus' important emphasis on reclaiming the lost sheep of Israel, the heart of his earthly mission. Week 3 then explores parables of God's mercy, including the parable of the good Samaritan. Week 4 relates to a set of parables in Luke that address the question of worldly wealth. Week 5 is a group of parables on the theme of Jesus' invitation, both those who accept it and reject it. Finally, week 6 is a collection of parables having to do with the final judgment.

Within each week, there are five days of reflection, looking at a parable or part of a parable each day. The aim is to experience life transformation by hearing Jesus speak to you through the words he spoke to the Galilean Jews in the countryside, as well as through the way God inspired the gospel writers to mold that teaching for their own contexts and audiences several decades later. Hear God speak to you through Scripture and then live faithfully to his Word through the power of the Holy Spirit.

SEEDS AND WEEDS
Matthew 13; Mark 4

Others, like seed sown on good soil, hear the word,
accept it, and produce a crop—some thirty, some sixty,
some a hundred times what was sown.

—MARK 4:20

Day 1

BAD SOIL
Mark 4:1–7, 14–19

INTRODUCTION

The parable of the seeds, also called the parable of the sower or the parable of the soils, in a way is key to all of Jesus' parables. In Mark especially, only those who have "ears to hear" will understand and respond appropriately to Jesus' stories.

ENGAGE

There is only one sower and one type of seed in this story, but there are four different kinds of results. What accounts for the different results in each case is the soil. The first three kinds of soil are "bad soil." The first soil is really no soil at all, but seed falls on a path where birds quickly eat it up; the seed does not have a chance. The second soil is over rock and the seed has no room to lay down roots; the sun scorches it. The third soil has weeds in it that choke the good seed. Only in the final instance does the seed find soil where it can truly thrive.

EXAMINE

The first three soils represent three different responses to the Word, which surely is the good news about the kingdom of God (Mark 1:14–15). Those who are like the seed on the path that the birds eat are people who have no interest in spiritual things whatsoever. Any word about Christ or the good news goes in one ear and out the other. Trying to talk to them about God is like talking to a wall. Those who are like the rocky soil have no depth to their faith. They are enthusiastic when nothing is demanded but wither quickly when following Christ becomes difficult. The third kind of bad soil are people who become distracted by the worries of life or, alternatively, by success.

EXPLORE

Those like seed on the path would not likely read a book of this sort or listen to someone who is reading it. But if perhaps you have a faint glimmer of desire for God somewhere deep within, pray that the Lord will increase it! Those whose faith is superficial might best pray for God to deepen it before any time of trial might come. Our responses to times of trial often reveal how deep our roots have been in the time leading up to them. We have a choice whether wealth or desires for other things choke out God. In such cases, we must insist on leaving time for God. In the worries of life, we must continually turn to God for help.

God's grace that comes to us at first brings our first wish to please God, the first dawn of light concerning his will, and the first ever so slight and passing conviction that we have sinned against him.

—JOHN WESLEY, PARAPHRASE

PRAYER

Father, in your grace lead me to hear your words, deepen my faith, and make room for you. Keep me from slumbering in my faith.

Day 2

GOOD SOIL
Mark 4:8–13, 20

INTRODUCTION

After describing three different kinds of bad soil, Jesus went on to speak about the good soil, which represents not only those who hear the Word, but also accept it and then bear fruit in their lives.

ENGAGE

Good soil yields fruit. It is tempting in our current climate to interpret this growth as getting more and more people to come to our churches. Certainly the New Testament at times models this sort of numerical growth. At other times, faithfulness only brings opposition and suffering. In the end, the kind of fruit that Jesus is most interested in has more to do with the fruit of righteousness.

It is a fruit that does no wrong to others (see Matt. 3:8) and helps those who are in need (see Matt. 25:31–46). It is the fruit of the Spirit (Gal. 5:22–23). When we yield this kind of fruit in our lives, others are drawn to Christ (Matt. 5:16).

The fruit of the Spirit is love, joy, peace, forbearance, kindness, goodness, faithfulness, gentleness and self-control.

—GALATIANS 5:22–23

EXAMINE

Sometimes we like to think of the parables as good illustrations, as stories that make it easier for us to understand Jesus' message. The book of Mark does not present the parables in this way. We might think of parables for Mark more as riddles. They function to filter out those who do not have faith as they listen "so that 'they may be ever seeing but never perceiving'" (Mark 4:12). Ironically, the disciples did not even understand this parable about the soils. Jesus wondered how they would understand any parable when they could not even understand the parable whose point was that only those with faith would understand his parables! Jesus showed mercy on them and revealed the parable's meaning anyway.

EXPLORE

We should be in awe of the grace of God that not only gives us "ears to hear," but even stoops to our weakness when we are hard of hearing. The words of the father in Mark 9:24 shout out to us: "Help me overcome my unbelief!" The disciples were not far enough in faith to understand Jesus' parable, but they wanted to understand. Jesus met them where they were and took them further in maturity and discipleship. We can go a long time without realizing we are not hearing well or that we are not seeing clearly. Sometimes God or life jolts us from our faith slumber. It would be better for us to make ourselves stop and take stock of our hearing.

PRAYER

Father, give me a true sense of where I am in my faith journey; then take me to the next level in maturity.

Day 3

PULLING THE WEEDS
Matthew 13:24–30, 36–43

INTRODUCTION

The book of Matthew alone has the parable of the weeds. It relates to the fact that believers live among unbelievers and the unfaithful. Some of the unfaithful may even look like the faithful.

ENGAGE

In the parable of the weeds, the Devil mixes his own children in with those who are truly members of the kingdom of God. In the current age, the Lord allows the two to coexist in the same field together, until the time of harvest at the end of the age. Then those who were not the true wheat, the weeds, will be gathered together and burned. The identity of the weeds is a little ambiguous.

They are the world that surrounds believers (Matt. 13:38), which includes a lot of people who have nothing to do with the church. But the idea of the weeds creeping in after the Word is sown makes us think of individuals mixed into the church.

EXAMINE

At a number of points, Matthew has striking statements and images that told his audience that not everyone who called him- or herself a believer was really part of the kingdom of God. Jesus said something similar at the end of the Sermon on the Mount—not everyone who will say, "Lord, Lord" to him on the day of judgment will be included (Matt. 7:21–23). Jesus also said something similar in the parable of the sheep and the goats— some will be surprised that they are not in the kingdom (Matt. 25:41–46). In the parable of the weeds, it seems that alongside those worshiping in the early church are also some who are weeds, destined for burning. For now, God leaves them alone.

EXPLORE

It is unnerving to know that some who think they are God's favorites may not actually be in the kingdom of God at all. One reason we can be deceived is because of how easy it is to confuse our culture with Christ. For example, many American Christians probably cannot tell the difference between patriotism and Christianity. Others have difficulty telling the difference between the values of their political party and Jesus' values. Sometimes we cannot tell the difference between what our denomination or church thinks and what the Bible really teaches. We need to have a reality check on *God's* values: Do we love our enemies? Are we fully surrendered to God's will, no matter what he would ask?

Jesus replied: "'Love the Lord your God with all your heart and with all your soul and with all your mind.' This is the first and greatest commandment. And the second is like it: 'Love your neighbor as yourself.' All the Law and the Prophets hang on these two commandments."

—MATTHEW 22:37–40

PRAYER

Father, save me from my own self-deception. Jolt me from thinking I am good seed if that is not the case. Help me embrace your values.

Day 4

SURPRISING GROWTH
Mark 4:26–34

INTRODUCTION

These verses give two of the shorter parables. The first is the parable of the growing seed (Mark 4:26–29). The second is the more familiar parable of the mustard seed (4:30–32).

ENGAGE

The parable of the growing seed is similar in some ways to the parable of the soils, but shorter. We can imagine that Jesus told these sorts of stories more than once and probably changed them a little here and there to suit different audiences. In this simile, Jesus compared the kingdom of God to some seed that has been scattered and continues to grow whether anyone is watching it or not. Whether the man who scattered the seed pays attention or not, the seed is growing. To the one who is watching, you can see first the stalk come up. Then the head comes up. Finally, the kernel of grain shows up.

EXAMINE

The parable of the mustard seed is another comparison between the kingdom of God and a seed. A mustard seed is very small, even if it is not the smallest seed that exists. But its size, when it grows, is completely disproportional to its beginning. Birds can even perch in its branches. We tend to think of crowds gathering around Jesus. But it is possible that at the very beginning, his ragtag group of followers might have felt pretty small compared to all Israel. And they were only in the north, the back hills of what used to be the kingdom of Israel. This parable might have been an encouragement to them, to wait and see just how big the movement would become.

I planted the seed, Apollos watered it,
but God has been making it grow.

—1 CORINTHIANS 3:6

EXPLORE

Both of these short similes remind us, first, that God is the one who brings the increase of the kingdom and, second, that small beginnings can lead to something huge over time. Paul would later remind the Corinthian church of the first truth: God is the one who makes things grow — at least as far as true growth is concerned (1 Cor. 3:7). So these parables are not a call to inaction. God expects us to be diligent and work hard for the growth of the kingdom. But we can only take the credit for being faithful, not for the growth. And God brings the growth in his own timing. In some instances, we may not see the full fruits in our lifetimes.

PRAYER

Father, let me be faithful and patient as I wait for you to bring the increase in your own good time.

Day 5

NETS AND TREASURES
Matthew 13:44–50

INTRODUCTION

Matthew's "parable sermon" (Matt. 13) includes several brief comparisons not found in the other Gospels. The parable of the net (13:47–50) is similar to the parable of the weeds. Then the parables of the hidden treasure and the pearl picture the great value of the kingdom.

ENGAGE

In the parable of the net, a net gathers a mixed collection of fish, some good and some bad. Right now, they are all mixed together. But when the net is full, at the end of the age, the angels will sort out the fish. The "bad fish" will be thrown into the fire of Gehenna, "where there will be weeping and gnashing of teeth" (13:50).

This image of hellfire, weeping, and wailing is a repeated image in Matthew. It comes straight out of the Jewish apocalyptic literature of the time and points to serious consequences for those who are not found to be right-eous on the day of judgment.

EXAMINE

One of the unique features of Matthew is that it often has "kingdom of heaven" where Mark and Luke have "kingdom of God." The two expressions probably mean the same basic thing. It would be easy to think Matthew was talking about going to heaven when he used the phrase "kingdom of heaven." But he was only referring to heaven as the place from which the kingdom is ruled. Heaven is the place from which God rules, so it is the kingdom *of heaven*. Some think calling it the kingdom of heaven showed reverence to God by not saying his name but the place from which he rules. Matthew, Mark, and Luke all seem to picture that eternal kingdom being on a renewed earth.

EXPLORE

The parable of the hidden treasure (Matt. 13:44) and the pearl (13:45–46) both highlight how important the kingdom of heaven is. Like the parable of the mustard seed, the hidden treasure and pearl are small. Most people do not notice or find them. This is no doubt how so many of the early Christian Jews must have felt, including Jesus' own disciples. We often have the luxury today of feeling like Christianity is the majority. But these parables are a reminder that even if the entire world was against us or demeaned what we believe, our faith and the kingdom to which we belong is more precious than all the fish in the net. God and his kingdom are worth our all.

PRAYER

Jesus, help me to see that following you is worth my all, my everything. Let me never take your kingdom for granted.

Only one life, 'twill soon be past, only what's done for Christ will last.

—C. T. STUDD

BRIDGING JESUS' WORLD AND OURS

Even if the meaning of Jesus' parables may at times have eluded the hardhearted in the crowds, these short stories and comparisons reach out to us across the centuries. The people in the world around us, the other fish in the net with us, look a lot different. But we are still the people of God, living in a world where there are pretenders and outright evil. It is still God who causes true growth. The kingdom has already become a massive tree in which birds from all the nations perch, although we still look for the kingdom to come in its fullness. The kingdom of God is still the greatest treasure we can hope to find.

Which kind of seed are you? Are you listening to God? Are you putting down roots in Christ by spending time with him and his people? Are you letting the cares of the world—or its prosperity—crowd God out of your life? Or are you growing? Can others see the difference in you since you started your faith? Is it a good difference?

EXERCISE

This next week, whenever you open your Bible, set aside time to pray or go to worship or fellowship with others. Pause for a moment and remember how valuable a prize God has given us to be part of his kingdom.

Week 2

PRODIGALS AND THE LOST
Matthew 21; Luke 15

Bring the fattened calf and kill it. Let's have a
feast and celebrate. For this son of mine was dead
and is alive again; he was lost and is found.

—LUKE 15:23–24

Day 1

THE TWO SONS
Matthew 21:28–32

INTRODUCTION

This short parable probably had a very similar meaning to the longer parable of the prodigal son. The two sons represent two different reactions to Jesus' ministry: the tax collectors and prostitutes, who started wrong but were ending more right than the religious leaders of Israel.

ENGAGE

We are so used to thinking of the religious leaders of Jesus' day as the bad guys that it is hard for us to remember that they were usually the ones who were revered and respected as holy by those in Israel. Like the one son in this parable, they started out saying they would work in the field. But then God sent John the Baptist to show them the way of righteousness. They did not accept John or his message. And when they saw the tax collectors and prostitutes repenting and changing, they still did not believe. All the law-keeping they had done did not matter when they rejected God's purpose and plan.

*Do you not know that in a race all the runners
run, but only one gets the prize?
Run in such a way as to get the prize.*

— 1 CORINTHIANS 9:24

EXAMINE

In no way did Jesus affirm the sins of tax collectors and prostitutes, just as he did not affirm the starting point of the son who initially said he would not go work. Jesus only affirmed the fact that they repented. God sent John the Baptist to show Israel that it was full of sin and needed to repent. The tax collectors and prostitutes listened and they changed for Jesus. We believe as Christians that such change was not something they could do in their own power, just as we believe that more law-observant Jews like the temple priests were also sinners. But the prostitutes availed themselves of God's power to change, while the leaders did not.

EXPLORE

The goal for believers is both to say yes to work in God's field and to actually go and do the work. Probably the biggest lesson here for Christians is the fact that it is not enough simply to say that we will go "work in the field." Those of us born into Christian families and have grown up going to church can deceive ourselves that it is enough to say we are believers, like so many of the religious leaders of Jesus' day. We think it is enough just to do the things we were raised to do. But we must truly listen *and* truly follow. The prize goes to those who finish the race, not to those who only begin.

PRAYER

Jesus, shake me from any sense I might have that it is enough merely to say I am your follower.

Day 2

THE LOST SHEEP AND COIN
Luke 15:1–10

INTRODUCTION

Luke 15 has three parables, all of which in their own way show that God is deeply concerned with those who have gone astray. The first two are the parables of the lost sheep and the lost coin.

ENGAGE

Jesus' priority in his earthly mission seemed to have been the "lost sheep" and the "lost coin." Jesus did not run his earthly mission on the model of "all have sinned" and therefore all must be reclaimed. He started with the assumption that the religious leaders were actually trying to follow God and the law. He talked of them, at least initially, as the "healthy" who did not need a doctor (see

Luke 5:31; Matt. 9:12). Of course, they would end up as the lost, and many of those who were initially lost would be reclaimed. In the end, most religious leaders did not repent. But in the Gospels, they align with "the righteous" (see Luke 5:32).

EXAMINE

The original context of Jesus' sayings was Israel. People were "born into" Israel. In that sense, being faithful to God for a Jew was more about *staying* in the people of God than *getting* in. A lost sheep or lost coin in that sense referred to a Jew who should have been part of God's people by default, but who even under such ideal circumstances found themselves separated from God. We also should not miss the element of rejoicing that is in these parables. When the lost sheep and the lost coin is found, God throws a party to celebrate. Part of the family has been reclaimed. Even the angels get involved with the celebration.

EXPLORE

Many in the church have children who are lost, even though they were born into Christian families and were raised to love the Lord. How troubling to know that they once knew the way and maybe even started down the path but went astray and lost their direction. As Christians, we know from Paul that "all have sinned" and thus that even those who have never known of Christ are lost and that God wants to draw all humanity back to himself. These parables of the lost seem to indicate that reclaiming the lost is the church's first order of business. Imagine if we were to seek them as diligently as this poor woman searching for a valuable coin!

Rescue the perishing, care for the dying, snatch them in pity from sin and the grave; weep o'er the erring one, lift up the fallen, tell them of Jesus, the mighty to save.

—FANNY CROSBY

PRAYER

Spirit, give me eyes to see the lost and a heart to yearn for their return like the woman searching for her lost coin.

Day 3

THE PRODIGAL
Luke 15:11–19

INTRODUCTION

The parable of the prodigal son has three main characters, and each of them teaches us a significant lesson. The one we usually remember the most is the Prodigal Son, the one who runs away from his father.

ENGAGE

The Prodigal, or lost son, more or less tells his father that he wishes his father were dead. A number of elements in this story would have had clear meanings in ancient Israel. For example, the fact that the Prodigal finds himself in a place where they have pigs clearly indicates that he has left Israel. Jews did not eat pork and would not have had pigs. This fact suggests that the Prodigal has not only left his village, but he has also left his people altogether. And since Yahweh, the God of Israel, is centered on earth in the land of Israel, this Prodigal has, in a real sense, abandoned God as well. His god is pleasure.

Though they are slighting him, still he is waiting,
waiting the penitent child to receive; plead
with them earnestly, plead with them gently;
he will forgive if they only believe.

—Fanny Crosby

EXAMINE

The family was incredibly important in the ancient world. It was your family you could count on for safety. It was your family that protected you when you were a child and your family that took care of you when you were old. The father was clearly the center of power and authority in the ancient family and respect for the older members of a family was also a central feature. Among the children, the firstborn son had the most authority and privilege. It is hard for most of us to imagine the shame the Prodigal Son brought to his father by, in effect, willfully acting out his death. He disregarded the most central values of his culture for selfish reasons.

EXPLORE

It was pleasure, more than anything else, that seemed to have tempted the lost son away from his family, his people, and his God. Money was a means to that pleasure. It is true that the elder brother is the one who says the younger has wasted his father's property on prostitutes, but the story probably wants us to assume that this statement is true. How easily this story reaches across time! Has any place or time in history been more allured by pleasure, money, and sex than the last century of American history? The Prodigal does not even seem to notice the offense he has brought to all around him. He is just thinking of himself and his own pleasure.

PRAYER

Jesus, make me a child who knows what is truly valuable and who is faithful, especially to the heavenly Father.

Day 4

THE OLDER BROTHER
Luke 15:25–30

INTRODUCTION

It is easy to forget the older brother in the parable of the prodigal son. But he also holds important lessons for some of us, especially those who have spent their whole lives doing their "duties" as Christians.

ENGAGE

It is easy to sympathize with the anger of the older brother. The students who are most likely to get angry when a teacher gives grace are those who have expended great effort in getting the assignment done or getting ready for the test. Imagine that you have been studying for a test all week. Imagine that you have spent dozens of hours in the library working on an assignment and writing it. Then let's say some students have been partying all week. They have had plenty of fun, and then have had plenty of sleep. Then imagine the professor letting them off the hook for the assignment or giving them some of the answers to the test. Wouldn't you be angry?

EXAMINE

We are so used to thinking of the Pharisees as obvious legalists and hypocrites that it is difficult for us to hear them as the audiences of Jesus and the Gospels would have. They were looked up to and were at least trying to keep the Old Testament law. We have promoted simplistic stories about crazy traditions they added to God's true requirements. There is no doubt a kernel of truth here, but we fail to examine ourselves. How many extra rules have we added over the years? You cannot do that on Sunday; you cannot wear this or do that. Many who promote these extra rules are at least trying to do the right thing and honor God in what they do.

EXPLORE

When we are trying hard to do the right thing, we can easily be tempted to begrudge those who get to cut in line. Why should those people get help from the government when I am working hard for my money? Why should we give a path to citizenship for those people when they came here illegally? We may not become angry with God directly, but we can become angry with people who favor these sorts of "liberal" notions. What we learn from the older brother is that God is in the business of reclaiming the lost. And what we learn from Paul is that we all are lost. At the end of the story, it is the older brother who has become the Prodigal.

Down in the human heart, crushed by the tempter,
feelings lie buried that grace can restore; touched
by a loving heart, wakened by kindness, chords
that were broken will vibrate once more.

—FANNY CROSBY

PRAYER

Spirit, soften my heart to love the Prodigal. Melt my heart that is so prone to begrudge those who receive mercy.

Day 5

THE FATHER
Luke 15:20–24, 31–32

INTRODUCTION

The father in the parable of the prodigal son tells us about what God the Father is like. He is eager to take the lost son back, and he even speaks lovingly to his disgruntled, older son.

ENGAGE

What a loving and forgiving father! First his younger son in effect wishes him dead, asking for the inheritance he would not normally receive until his father's death. Then when the son returns, he not only accepts him, but the old man disgraces himself by running. Perhaps he wishes to protect his son from the violence of the village. The father does not demean and punish his son as a slave; he celebrates. He gives him the ring off his finger and throws a feast. Then his older son dishonors him by questioning his authority to forgive. His older son disobeys him by refusing to come in. Even then, the father patiently and lovingly explains to the older son what he is doing.

The child asks of the Father whom he knows. . . . The right way to approach God is to stretch out our hands and ask of One who we know has the heart of a Father.

—Dietrich Bonhoeffer

EXAMINE

It is popular these days to view Christ's death in mathematical, legalistic terms. God demanded that someone pay the price for the sins of the world. Only a human could pay that penalty. The precise amount of sin had to be paid for. The idea of penal substitution is that Jesus took this precise punishment for the sins he atoned for. Otherwise we would be lost. Notice, however, that the parable of the prodigal son knows nothing of such math or legality. The father in the story, who represents God, has the authority to forgive his lost son outright.

For this reason, some scholars like to think of the father as a Prodigal, reckless father, just as God's love and forgiveness for us is "reckless."

EXPLORE

It will be tempting for some to think of the father in this parable as weak. Doesn't he let his younger son disgrace him? He even lets his older son talk back to him. They need to be punished. But this father is not weak. This father is more concerned for the destiny of his lost son than in his own dignity or pride. A lot of what passes for "Christian justice" is really moral immaturity and a weak heart. It takes strength to forgive when someone wrongs you. It is easy to get back at them or to disown them. That is not God's way.

PRAYER

Father, give me the strength to forgive like you. Give me the power to love others more than my own pride and dignity.

BRIDGING JESUS' WORLD AND OURS

Christian theology has broadened the sense of Jesus' parables of the lost. Whereas originally they had everything to do with the lost of Israel, we have appropriated Paul's inspired insight that "all have sinned" to lead us to the realization that we are all Prodigals. The default state of humanity is one of separation from God. We all start in the faraway country.

The older brothers today are no longer the religious leaders of Israel. Now they are people who have grown up in the church and come to see themselves as heirs. They are those who have forgotten that they once were Prodigals too. They are the ones who now are tempted to think that they deserve God's favor.

But the Father remains the same, ever willing to receive us, no matter how far we stray. The Father remains patient with the "older brothers" today, the ones that do not like it when visitors come to their churches who are not as holy and righteous-looking as they are. The Father remains biased toward mercy rather than punishment.

EXERCISE

Reflect on the parable of the prodigal son. Are you like the younger son? Do you need to come home? Are you like the older brother? Do you resent God's mercy and forgiveness to others? Resolve to come home or come into the house to celebrate.

GOD'S MERCY
Matthew 18:21–35; Luke 10, 18

"Which of these three do you think was a neighbor to the man who fell into the hands of robbers?" The expert in the law replied, "The one who had mercy on him." Jesus told him, "Go and do likewise."

—LUKE 10:36–37

Day 1

PRIESTS AND LEVITES
Luke 10:25–32

INTRODUCTION

The parable of the good Samaritan is one of the best-known of all Jesus' parables. Today we look at the priest and Levite in the story as people who are good at keeping the letter of the law but who miss the spirit of it.

ENGAGE

At various times, some have made a big deal about Christians believing in absolutes, where an absolute is a duty to which there is never an exception. We believe in absolutes. We believe that there is never a time to make an exception to love God with our whole heart or to love our neighbor as ourselves. But those who emphasize absolutes usually are emphasizing rules more like the ones the priest and Levite in this story apparently emphasized. The duty they should have emphasized was the importance of loving their neighbor. God desires mercy, not sacrifice, Scripture says (Hos. 6:6; Matt. 9:13). To save a life is more important to God than to stay "clean."

EXAMINE

We should not miss the fact that Jesus chose a priest and Levite to be the ones who passed by the mugged man. He did not pick a Pharisee for this story. What the priest and Levite both have in common is the fact that they are people whose Old Testament role involved a high degree of concern about purity. The priest is traveling from Jerusalem to Jericho. Perhaps he has just completed some sort of service in the temple. Perhaps he is concerned to stay pure because it is his week to serve, and he is supposed to return the next day. Jesus left such things to our imagination. But the story clearly embodies the priority of mercy over sacrifice—and over Old Testament purity.

EXPLORE

It is fascinating and troubling that Christians sometimes use the Scriptures to try to get around the most important things God calls us to do. In this case, the priest and Levite were presumably hiding behind the letter of Scripture in order to violate its heart. How many of those who argued for slavery in the mid-1800s used the letter of Scripture to justify it? How many today use the letter of Scripture as a tool to keep women out of leadership in the church? How many today use the idea of God's justice as an excuse to oppress or get out of mercy toward others? God is not fooled. He blesses the merciful. They are the ones who receive his mercy.

I love your Christ; I do not like your Christians.

—Mahatma Gandhi

PRAYER

Spirit, protect me from self-deception. Protect me from tricking myself into thinking that you prize justice over mercy.

Day 2

GOOD SAMARITANS
Luke 10:33–37

INTRODUCTION

The hero of the parable is a Samaritan, exactly the type of person the expert in the law did not want to be his neighbor. In answer to his question of who his neighbor truly was, Jesus picked one of the people the expert would least want it to be.

ENGAGE

The expert in the law had all the marks of the worst kind of lawyer—someone who knows how to use the minutia and loopholes of the law in order to get out of doing the right thing. The expert knew the heart of God's law perhaps better than most of us. "Love God and love neighbor," he correctly responded. But he was a clever lawyer. He wanted to define *neighbor* in a way that fit with what he wanted to be true. He wanted his neighbor to be people he liked, people who shared his values. He did not want his neighbor to be sinners, people who had faulty theology, or people who did not live the way he thought they should live.

The first question which the priest and the Levite asked was: "If I stop to help this man, what will happen to me?" But . . . the Good Samaritan reversed the question: "If I do not stop to help this man, what will happen to him?"

—MARTIN LUTHER KING, JR.

EXAMINE

Even from Jesus' perspective, the Samaritans had the wrong theology and the wrong ethics. They were the people who lived in between Judea in the south where Jerusalem was and Galilee in the north where Jesus grew up. It was an area that was once part of Israel. It was also an area that was less careful about marrying non-Israelites, and its form of Judaism mixed more with pagan religion. They even had a different version of the law.

They did not believe, for example, that the Jerusalem temple was the right temple. By choosing a Samaritan to be the hero, Jesus was saying that we must love everyone, even our enemies. There are no exceptions.

EXPLORE

Christians sometimes try to justify hatred for others by hiding behind disagreements in theology or practice. We may not even admit that it is hatred, but we can act rudely or offensively without even thinking of it: They're Catholic; they're homosexual; they're Muslim; they're Calvinist or Arminian; they're liberal or conservative. God does not expect us to change our beliefs or convictions for others, but he expects us to act lovingly toward everyone. God even expects us to act in hope of the redemption of murderers. We may not always feel warmly toward those we, by God's grace, act lovingly toward. Love is not about how we feel; love is about how we choose to act toward others.

PRAYER

Lord, uncover my secret motives and true intentions. Once I see them for what they are, help me do what I must.

Day 3

THE UNFORGIVING SERVANT
Matthew 18:21–35

INTRODUCTION

Today we continue the theme of God's merciful nature by looking at the parable of the unforgiving servant in Matthew 18. Peter asked Jesus how many times he should forgive someone who wronged him. Jesus' answer, in effect, was "every time."

ENGAGE

When Peter asked this question, Jesus had been talking not only about literal children, but also about the "little ones" in the church (see 18:1–11), those who are led by Christian leaders. Those who lead people in the church astray are in grave danger of God's coming judgment. Next comes Matthew's version of the parable of the lost sheep, reflecting God's great desire to bring the lost back. Verses 15–20 then give the classic text about confronting those who do wrong in the church. It is at this point that we find the parable of the unforgiving servant. What if the person who has done wrong repents? It is human nature not to forgive them but instead to long for their punishment.

EXAMINE

Many of the parables and metaphors in the Bible are like proverbs. They give a glimpse or snapshot of the truth, but not the entire picture. Psalm 103:12 says that God puts our sins as far away as the east is from the west, and Isaiah 43:25 says God does not remember our sins any longer after he blots them out. These pictures need to be balanced with the parable of the unforgiving servant. In this story, all the debts of the unforgiving servant are first eliminated by his master, who represents God. Then all those debts come back again, because the servant, to whom God has shown such an immense grace, refuses to show the same graciousness to someone else who owes him hardly anything.

EXPLORE

"All have sinned." We get it with our heads. No one deserves God's grace or has earned God's approval. It is a free gift. God is graciously willing to forgive all the wrongs we have ever done. But we can also insult his grace (see Heb. 10:29). The parable of the unforgiving servant is both a picture of God's grace and his expectations of us, if we are to receive it. First, he is willing to forgive us any amount of wrongdoing we have done, and we all owe him more than we could possibly repay. But he expects us to forgive and give grace to those who wrong us as well, and nothing another person does to us can compare to our debt to God.

Blessed are the merciful,
for they will be shown mercy.

—MATTHEW 5:7

PRAYER

Father, first give me a sense of the magnitude of what I owe you, then help me remember my indebtedness when I go to forgive others.

Day 4

THE PERSISTENT WIDOW
Luke 18:1–8

INTRODUCTION

One of the special features of Luke's gospel is the respect he paid to women. This parable said to its ancient audiences that, if even a widow might receive the attention of a heartless judge, imagine the attention we will receive from a God who loves us.

ENGAGE

As much as Americans in particular complain about our government and judicial system, we are in much better shape than most people in most times and places in history. The parable of the persistent widow pictures a judge who could not care less whether he is liked by God or anyone else (18:4). He is not interested in the problems of some widow, who lived as one of the more powerless members of ancient society. With her husband dead, this widow apparently has no one to keep other men—perhaps even the family of her dead husband—from taking advantage of her weakness. The judge does not care, but her persistence is finally enough to get him to give in and bring justice.

Real prayer comes not from gritting our teeth but from falling in love.

—Richard Foster

EXAMINE

Not every element of a parable is part of the point. So in this particular parable, the judge is absolutely not meant to give us a direct picture of God. God is not like some self-preoccupied judge who is not really interested in us. God is not too busy for us, so that the only way we can ever get his attention is by constantly bugging him until we finally wear him down. The point is that even a wicked judge would bring justice eventually if someone persisted long enough. God is not wicked but eager to bring us justice. Also, a widow would be easy for a judge to ignore, since she is practically powerless, but even the weakest person is meaningful to God.

EXPLORE

The point of the parable is that we should not give up crying out for justice night and day. Why God does not always answer us instantly is a mystery. God knows what we need and when we need it. Indeed, he knows far better than we do what is for the best. Persistence in prayer is a good thing for us. God does not need it, but it focuses our faith. It cooperates with God's will. It strengthens our resolve and ability to endure. We can all go to God, as long as our hearts are truly longing for his will. And he will always bring justice. It may not come today, but come it will, if not now, in eternity.

PRAYER

Father, strengthen me to keep praying, even when it looks as if the wicked will prevail. Give me the calm assurance that you are still in control.

Day 5

THE PHARISEE AND
THE TAX COLLECTOR
Mark 11:1–6

INTRODUCTION

We end this week of God's mercy with the parable of the Pharisee and the tax collector, also unique to Luke's gospel. Like the widow, the tax collector stands powerless before God, with nothing to offer but his sincere and absolute repentance.

ENGAGE

We are so used to the Pharisees being the bad guys that it is hard for us to hear this parable as those who first heard it likely did. The Pharisees were generally loved by the people of Israel, and they were deeply respected for their godliness. Jesus' audience was probably shocked to hear that God favored the tax collector instead. Some

Pharisees were apparently too confident in their own righteousness. The Pharisee of this parable does not have the proper respect for the graciousness of God. We can imagine that the apostle Paul was a little like this Pharisee before Christ gently corrected him. Paul had been blameless, at least as far as a person could keep the law (Phil. 3:6).

EXAMINE

Like the Prodigal Son, the tax collector in this parable knows that he has been a blatant sinner. For this reason, he knows that he is completely dependent on God's mercy. He does not even venture to look into heaven because he realizes he has no grounds to ask for God's grace. If he is a typical tax collector, he has not only inflicted on poor people the economic abuse of those above him, but he will also have added a little extra on top for his own pockets. Jesus once again turns the expectations and values of his audience on its head. This despicable man, because he is truly repentant, is the one whose prayers God accepts.

EXPLORE

The capacity of the human heart to twist even righteousness for evil is astounding. Here is a Pharisee who we should admire for the way he tithes and fasts. But he turns it into something that creates a barrier between him and God. Have you ever known people who took pride in being humble? Have you ever known anyone who was proud of the fact that they did not wear jewelry or that their hair was long and natural instead of short and dyed? The human heart can take our acts of obedience and try to turn them into self-sufficiency and divine merit. But all that counts before God is a heart truly surrendered to him. He loves the good works we do from this sort of heart.

PRAYER

Father, may I do any act of righteousness with a heart of gratefulness that you even give me the chance to serve you.

When you see a man with a great deal of religion displayed in his shop window, you may depend upon it, he keeps a very small stock of it within.

—CHARLES H. SPURGEON

BRIDGING JESUS' WORLD AND OURS

God's values of mercy and compassion are timeless. We find them in the way God approached Nineveh in the Old Testament (see Jon. 4:2). We find it in the teaching of James, Paul, and John. We certainly find it in the teaching of Jesus. The parables this week give us just the smallest reminder of how central mercy was to Jesus' earthly message.

"Mercy triumphs over judgment," James 2:13 says. It is not a teaching without complication. What of hell and eternal damnation? What of the cross and the satisfaction of God's justice? These are great questions. But they are questions for God, not for us.

For us, we are to "leave room for God's wrath" (Rom. 12:19). That is to say, as individuals, God calls us to show mercy and let God take care of the justice. As individuals, God calls us to forgive as many times as a person genuinely repents. God calls us to help those in need, even if they do not deserve it. God and governments can worry about justice. We are to worry about mercy.

EXERCISE

Think back over this week. Were there any times when you had the opportunity to show someone mercy? Did you? Were there any instances when someone wanted your forgiveness? Did you give it? You know what God wants you to do. You only need to do it.

MONEY AND THE KINGDOM
Luke 12, 16

No one can serve two masters. Either you will hate
the one and love the other, or you will be devoted
to the one and despise the other. You cannot
serve both God and money.

—LUKE 16:13

Day 1

THE RICH FOOL
Luke 12:13–21

INTRODUCTION

Luke's gospel is particularly negative toward money and the wealthy. In the parable of the rich fool, Jesus told of a man who has no thought for God's values and plans, but thinks only of his own ambitions.

ENGAGE

The rich fool in this parable has a number of problems. For one, he has scarcely given a thought to God's plan for the future. He is focused on himself and on accruing more things. He is not laying up treasures for himself in heaven but laying up treasures for himself on earth, where moth and rust corrupt (see Matt. 6:19–20). He wants to set himself up for a nice retirement, where he can take his excess grain and never have to work again the rest of his days. He does not seem to give God the credit for his success or give God thanks. His imminent death is an indication that God's plan ultimately trumps our planning.

God, grant me the serenity to accept the things
I cannot change, the courage to change the things
I can, and the wisdom to know the difference.

—Reinhold Niebuhr

EXAMINE

Jesus told this parable because someone in the crowd wanted him to intervene in a family dispute. The man, presumably a younger brother, wanted Jesus to tell his older brother to do the right thing. But Jesus knew that God's kingdom was coming and those concerns were passing away. It is striking that Jesus associated such seemingly legitimate concerns with greed. "Life does not consist in an abundance of possessions" (Luke 12:15). Rather, we should share any excess we have with those who are in need. It seems Jesus faulted the man in the parable because he is not interested in sharing his abundance with others. The man has much more than he needs to live. He should give it away.

EXPLORE

God is the one in charge. Have you ever had someone make a decision that was really yours to make? Human nature, especially for those who are insecure, drives the urge to squash the usurper in such situations. Of course God is not insecure. He often must sit back and smile—or shake his head—as we go around planning our lives as if we are in control, as if we control the outcome. Surrendering to God's plan and will is difficult. Certainly God wants us to do what we can. Surely he does not want us just sitting around. But he is the ultimate decider, and we should live with a sense that all of our plans are if "it is the Lord's will" (James 4:15).

PRAYER

Father, I surrender my future to you, thankful for all the good you have given me. I submit my life to your will and plan.

Day 2

LAZARUS THE BEGGAR
Luke 16:19–23

INTRODUCTION

We can tell by the way Jesus introduced the story of the rich man and Lazarus that it is a parable and not a story about the Lazarus who Jesus raised from the dead in the gospel of John. The Lazarus of this story has no home.

ENGAGE

Lazarus lies at the gate of the rich man, hoping that he might get some scraps left over from the feasting at the rich man's house. Presumably the dogs that lick Lazarus's sores also survive on those scraps. Perhaps the dogs are meant to show just how low Lazarus has sunk in the world. Are we meant to think that the dogs get more of the rich man's scraps than Lazarus does? Do the dogs have more pity on him than the unnamed rich man himself does? It is not clear how Lazarus arrives at the rich man's gate since, presumably, he can hardly walk. Meanwhile, we get the impression that the rich man does not give him a thought, although he must pass him when he leaves his house.

EXAMINE

Jesus said, "Blessed are you who are poor. . . . Blessed are you who hunger now. . . . But woe to you who are rich, for you have already received your comfort. Woe to you who are well fed now, for you will go hungry" (Luke 6:20–21, 24–25). These values underlie this parable. The parable says nothing about Lazarus being virtuous or the rich man being evil. It merely acts out these beatitudes. Those who are hungry now will be rich later, and those who are rich now will be hungry later. We immediately want to make qualifications, and we probably can. Perhaps it is not that simple. But we should live with the words in their starkness for a few moments before we start our qualifications.

EXPLORE

We are prone to make excuses for why we might pay no attention to the homeless on the street: "It's his own fault; he could get a job or go on welfare. Those beggars probably have more money than I do." Our hearts can be hard, and we can even trick ourselves into thinking we are actually righteous to be angry at such "dirty" people. Jesus just did not agree. There is no way around him. When we were his enemies, he reached out to help us. Whatever the causes of such destitution, what matters is that we have compassion and an earnest desire to see them lifted from the mire—even if we see their destitution as their own doing.

*It is one of the most beautiful compensations
of this life that no man can sincerely try to
help another without helping himself.*

—RALPH WALDO EMERSON

PRAYER

Jesus, shatter my hard heart of stone and replace it with a soft heart of compassion, even for those who do not want it.

Day 3

THE RICH MAN IN TORMENT
Luke 16:24–31

INTRODUCTION

Yesterday we looked at Lazarus and his situation. Today we focus on the rich man and his fate. The rich man ends up in torment in Hades, desperately hoping someone will go back to warn his family of the fate that awaits them too.

ENGAGE

The reversal of Lazarus's fortunes leaves him at Abraham's side, where he is comforted after his destitute life on earth. The rich man, by contrast, now finds himself in agony. When he was alive, the rich man dressed in purple and fine linen. Now he finds himself in a fire, ironically begging Lazarus for a drop of cool water.

There is a chasm between the two fates, and their destinies are sealed. It is a parable, so we cannot be sure that God wants us to take every element literally. But Christians throughout the ages have generally taken the story to mean that once we die, we cannot change locations. God does not even allow those with compassion to help those suffering after death.

Since, then, you have been raised with Christ,
set your hearts on things above, where Christ is,
seated at the right hand of God. Set your minds
on things above, not on earthly things.

—COLOSSIANS 3:1–2

EXAMINE

Most of the parable does not have a particularly Jewish feel, but it is clear that both the rich man and Lazarus are Jews. The rich man calls Abraham his father, and Lazarus finds himself with Abraham in the afterlife. Abraham tells the rich man that his living brothers have the Old Testament Scriptures—of Moses and the Prophets—which implies that they are Jews. Abraham implies that the Law and the Prophets teach that God's people should take care of the poor among them, a teaching the rich man himself ignored while he was alive. Abraham tells the rich man in effect that people believe what they want to believe, and his family enjoys their life of luxury just fine as it is.

EXPLORE

Are we willing to change our minds and consider that we may be living wrongly? We can be so sure we know what is right that we will not even entertain the possibility that we are off track. The rich man's family was not interested in hearing that their lives were going in the wrong direction. They were only interested in the life of luxury and pleasure they were leading. Given how many contradictory things Christians teach, it is certain that many Christians are wrong about a lot of things. We all have misunderstood God's will and the Bible at some points. Are we willing to have God teach us? He will not be sending anyone back from the dead.

PRAYER

Spirit, steer my heart in the right direction. Don't let me get away with excuses and rationalizations out of step with your path.

Day 4

THE DISHONEST MANAGER
Luke 16:1–9

INTRODUCTION

The parable of the shrewd manager is one of the most puzzling of all Jesus' parables. In it Jesus commended the cleverness of a manager who gives away his master's money in order to make friends for himself after he is fired.

ENGAGE

This parable gives the audience a glimpse of a different world than their own. This is evident from the punch line Jesus gave at the end of the story: "The people of this world are more shrewd in dealing with their own kind than are the people of the light" (16:8). This implies that the individuals in the parable are not Jews or believers.

They are people "of this world." Jesus commended the sharing of wealth with others and the cancellation of debts. And he seemed to commend the master, because the master is not troubled by losing possessions he did not really need in the first place. But Jesus presumably did not commend dishonest management or stealing from one's employer.

EXAMINE

Luke and Acts are two volumes of a series, both of which are addressed to Theophilus. It is possible that this is a symbolic name for a "lover of God." But it is just as likely that Theophilus was the patron who supported Luke while he researched and wrote these volumes. If so, it is possible to see in this strange parable a hint to Theophilus that he should use his wealth—for such a patron would almost certainly be well off—in order to help others, including those who were in his debt. Christians with worldly wealth should use their resources to gain friends among the needy and then be welcomed into eternal dwellings one day.

EXPLORE

Sometimes among Christians today you will hear the commandment not to steal applied to taxes or to using money without permission to help others. It is difficult to make sense of that interpretation of stealing in the light of the Gospels. Rather, "the earth is the Lord's, and everything in it" (1 Cor. 10:26). It is not an absolute, but the consistent message of the New Testament is that believers should share their abundance above what they need with others who are in need. In this parable, Jesus made a positive point by a secular context in which one person's excess is shared with others against his will. As Jesus followers, we should not need to be forced to help others with our excess.

Earn all you can; save all you can;
give all you can.

—JOHN WESLEY

PRAYER

Father, pry my hands off the abundance of resources you give me, the ones I want to use for my selfish pleasures and indulgences.

Day 5

GOD AND MONEY
Luke 16:10–15

INTRODUCTION

In the verses immediately following the parable of the shrewd manager, Luke expanded on the significance of worldly wealth for believers, particularly believers with an abundance of wealth. They have God's property in their possession. What will they do with it?

ENGAGE

After the parable, Jesus reflected on the idea that God would not trust a person with much, great responsibility, unless he could trust the person with little responsibility. Cleverly, he put worldly wealth in the category of being entrusted with little. Perhaps Jesus was telling the Pharisees in his audience that God would not entrust them with the big task of the spiritual leadership of Israel because they had not been faithful with the "little" task of having worldly wealth. Serving God is a significant task. In Jesus' eyes, being entrusted with wealth is a little task. Meanwhile, God knew their hearts, just as God knows ours. He knows who we truly serve.

The LORD gave and the LORD has taken away;
may the name of the LORD be praised.

—JOB 1:21

EXAMINE

One important implication of Jesus' comments is that there were believers who had wealth. Jesus talked about them as individuals who God had "trusted with much" (16:10). He meant material wealth, which Jesus obviously did not consider to be "true riches" (16:11). We can infer from the parable of the shrewd manager that good management of worldly wealth means, to a large extent, giving it away, using it for the benefit of others. Apparently, Pharisees tended to be from the wealthier class of Jews. This makes sense, because only the wealthy would normally have had much leisure time to study. The Pharisees sneered at Jesus' suggestion that their love of money indicated a spiritual problem.

EXPLORE

"You cannot serve both God and money" (16:13). It is a familiar saying. It also tends to go in one ear and out the other, like the seed that fell along the path and was immediately snatched away by birds. How attached to our money and possessions are those of us who have never desperately longed for the next paycheck or not known if we would ever get another? How angry are we when someone scratches our perfect cars or our stocks go down? Rather, we should think of all our possessions as God's, with us as mere stewards of them. Then our mind-set would be, "How would God like me to use his money today?"

PRAYER

Father, all I have, I give to you. It is yours anyway. But I acknowledge it and will use it however you ask me to.

BRIDGING JESUS' WORLD AND OURS

Perhaps no topic in Jesus' parables is more controversial today than his teaching on money—at least in America. We want to find a way for Jesus not to mean what he seems to have meant.

There probably are some significant differences between Jesus' world and ours today. Jesus' world was a farming one where they exchanged goods more than coinage. Accordingly, they stored goods more than money, and such goods were limited. They did not have the "American dream" that anyone could become rich by working hard enough. Rather, wealth was often thought of in terms of stealing. If one person had more, someone else must have less. But our motto seems to be, "You have to spend money to make money."

Nevertheless, we can still follow Jesus' principle of using any extra we have to help others. We can still keep in mind that all our resources belong to God, not to ourselves. God is not stealing from us if he insists we use our resources to help and serve others. And we should always yield to God's plan in all our plan-making. We are not really in control.

EXERCISE

Think back over how you have spent God's money this week. What portion of your income and resources did you use in service to God? Did you think of the "stuff" in your life more as your stuff or God's? Give everything to God.

ANSWERING GOD'S INVITATION
Matthew 20–22; Luke 14

Then he said to his servants, "The wedding banquet is ready,
but those I invited did not deserve to come. So go to the
street corners and invite to the banquet anyone you find."

—MATTHEW 22:8–9

Day 1

EVEN IF YOU'RE LATE
Matthew 20:1–16

INTRODUCTION

In the parable of the day laborers, Jesus again turned our sense of fairness upside down. God pays all the workers the same amount, even though they all work different amounts.

ENGAGE

The parable of the day laborers is similar in some respects to the parable of the prodigal son. Some workers start working in the morning and work all day. For their work, the landowner promises them an honest day's wage—a denarius. Later, when the landowner pays a denarius to those who have only worked an hour, those who have worked all day expect to get more. When they don't, they grumble. It's similar to the way the older brother grumbles that his prodigal brother was paying no price for his sins—and that he was getting no extra reward for his faithfulness. Generosity—or mercy or grace—is never fair. It is, by definition, undeserved.

EXAMINE

All the workers need work. None of the workers are able to survive without work. The workers in the story represent those who answer the call to follow the Lord. If you glance back at the end of Matthew 19, you can see that Jesus' disciples left everything to follow him (19:27). They all went to work. In a sense, they had come to the field late, with only an hour to go, yet they would be some of the first in the kingdom. Some in Israel, even though they had been trying to follow God more seriously than any fisherman, refused to work when Jesus came calling. They ended up last.

EXPLORE

There are at least two major takeaways from this story. The most important is to go to work when the master calls. He wants to give you the work of following him. Are you old? Answer the call. Are you young? Answer the call. If you truly want to follow Jesus, he will take you late, if that is when you come. A second

Day 2

THE FIRST INVITEES
Matthew 21:33–46

INTRODUCTION

The parable of the tenants is one of several in the Gospels that indict the leadership of Israel for rejecting Jesus. But more poignant for us today is the importance of being faithful to the charge God has given us.

ENGAGE

The tenants in this parable represent the leadership of Israel. They were the ones who, more than anyone else, brought about the crucifixion of Jesus. In the parable, the tenants throw the son of the landowner out of the vineyard and kill him. The parable points to a pattern that reaches back into the Old Testament, where Israel's leaders rejected the prophets as well. Throughout history, Israel beat, stoned, and sometimes killed the ones God sent to them. These tenants of the land of Israel—who were not the true owners—were destined to have the land taken away from them. Matthew indicated that Jesus was talking about the chief priests and the Pharisees—individuals who together made up the Jewish ruling council.

*A charge to keep I have, a God to glorify, a
never-dying soul to save and fit it for the sky.
To serve the present age, my calling to fulfill, O may
it all my powers engage to do my Master's will.*

—CHARLES WESLEY

EXAMINE

Jesus is the stone that the builders rejected, which has ended up as the cornerstone of the building, the most important stone of all. It is a reminder that things are not always as they seem. Those who seem to be in power from an earthly perspective are not always the ones destined to win or who God favors. In this case, the one they rejected was God himself come in the flesh. From all earthly appearances, it looked like the Romans, the high priest, and even the Sanhedrin were in control. Who would have questioned it at the time? Who would have thought that the man on the cross, who died in shame, was in fact the winner, the true heir of the land?

EXPLORE

We all are tenants of God's property. Some of us live on more of his property than others. Some of us are single and are stewards of everything our individual lives touch. Some of us have families to take care of for God. Still others are leaders of churches or organizations. In our entire spheres of influence, we are tenants of God's property. We are not our own; we "were bought at a price" (1 Cor. 6:20). God does not need any one of us to accomplish his will. If we do not do his work, he can easily use someone else. This happened with the first tenants of the land. May it never be true of us!

PRAYER

Father, teach me how to be a good steward of the land you have given me to tend until your return.

Day 3

EXCUSES NOT TO COME
Luke 14:15–24

INTRODUCTION

Luke's parable of the great banquet is similar to Matthew's parable of the wedding banquet. Both versions of this story may incorporate elements that spoke directly to Matthew and Luke's contemporary situation, as well as to Jesus' circumstances.

ENGAGE

A man, who surely represents God, prepares a banquet. He invites many guests, but they all make excuses not to come. One person wants to go see a field he bought. Another wants to try out some new oxen. A third just got married and has the preoccupations of a new spouse. Since his initial guests do not come, the man giving the feast invites the poor, crippled, and lame instead. Even then, more are invited from the highways and byways. In this parable, Jesus is surely saying that the kingdom of God is more important than land or property. He even seems to be saying that it is more important than family. Following Jesus is more important than anything else.

EXAMINE

There are similarities in this parable with the parable of the tenants. However, in this story, the focus is not on those who steward the land of Israel but with those who are invited to the celebration that will take place after Jesus is enthroned as king. The introduction to this parable is someone looking forward to the future feasting when the kingdom of God fully comes to earth. So these related parables indict the leaders of Israel, the initial tenants, and the initial invitees to the banquet. This particular parable also highlights one of Luke's special emphases, Jesus' compassion on the poor of Israel. Perhaps later readers of this story would have heard in the last invitees an allusion to the Gentiles.

EXPLORE

We all know what it means to make excuses. Sometimes we do it so that we will not hurt someone else's feelings. But more often we do it because we are covering up our own true motivations. The first two excuses sound that way: "I'd come but I just bought a field." "I just bought some oxen." So can't you look at the field tomorrow? You just don't want to come. But Jesus teaches in the verses immediately following that he trumps everything, even a spouse. He ultimately trumps our families and children and parents. He is more important than our own lives. God does not usually call us to choose between our spouse and him, but he must always be first.

He that is good for making excuses is
seldom good for anything else.

—BENJAMIN FRANKLIN

PRAYER

Jesus, may you be the first priority in my life, and may my love for all else be an expression of my love for you.

Day 4

ALL ARE INVITED
Matthew 22:1–10

INTRODUCTION

Matthew's parable of the wedding banquet is similar to Luke's in that it also involves a number of people who reject an invitation to an important banquet. But like the parable of the tenants, the invitees persecute the messengers.

ENGAGE

The king invites everyone to the banquet, but those who are first invited do not come. Those who refuse the king's messengers and even kill some almost certainly represent the leaders of Israel. At the time of Jesus, these would especially have been high priests and members of the Sanhedrin, like the Pharisees. Interestingly, after

God destroys them, the king then invites both the good and the bad to the wedding banquet. Does this statement fit with the sense we get multiple times in Matthew that not everyone in the church is truly good? It is nice to think that all are invited to God's feast, even if not everyone will be able to stay.

"Whoever" surely means me!

—J. EDWIN MCCONNELL, PARAPHRASE

EXAMINE

This parable may date the gospel of Matthew to the time after Jerusalem was destroyed in A.D. 70. Matthew adds a detail that is not in Luke's parable of the great banquet. The king sends his army, destroys those who persecuted his messengers, and burns their city. Many scholars think that this detail hints that Matthew saw the destruction of Jerusalem as God's judgment on Israel for rejecting his prophets and rejecting Jesus. Of course some later Christians have used imagery of this sort as fuel in the hatred of Jews. It is important for us to remember that those specific Jews were already punished for putting Jesus to death two thousand years ago.

We cannot find an excuse for persecuting Jews today in texts like these.

EXPLORE

There is something striking about the fact that God invites everyone to his banquet, even though he knows some will end up being kicked out. Matthew as a whole indicates that God casts his net wide. It is not that he has no expectations or will end up accepting everyone. Quite the contrary, Matthew has some of the strongest language of eternal punishment in the whole Bible. But everyone is invited. This is how we should look at others. It may look as though some people will never end up choosing God or living for Christ. But we must make sure everyone hears the invitation. We must communicate and show God's love to everyone whether they receive and respond to it or not.

PRAYER

Father, may I never give up on the possibility that someone might still make it into your kingdom, regardless of how unlikely it may look.

Day 5

DRESS APPROPRIATELY
Matthew 22:11–14

INTRODUCTION

The parable of the wedding banquet ends with a twist. Someone shows up at the banquet improperly dressed. The king then throws him outside into the darkness, where there is "weeping and gnashing of teeth" (22:13).

ENGAGE

The king has already sent an army to destroy the city of those who rejected his invitation to the wedding banquet, those who also mistreated and murdered his messengers. Then the king invites everyone. But some attend who are not properly dressed. They do not have wedding clothes. Those who are not properly dressed are the "bad" who were invited along with the good. Their end sounds even worse than the initial invitees who did not come. The initial invitees are only said to be destroyed when the king destroys their city. By contrast, those who come but are not fit are cast into the darkness, where there is weeping and gnashing of teeth, which in Matthew seems to refer to hellfire (see 13:42).

EXAMINE

In several of the parables, some end up coming to the banquet who are not truly "in." What must the church of Matthew's day have looked like for him to have this strong theme in his gospel? Suffice it to say, Matthew surely believed that not everyone worshiping in the churches of his day was truly part of the kingdom. Some prophets, some exorcists, some wealthy, maybe he had in mind some Gentile converts—they may have thought they were "in," but God thought otherwise. They were doing some of the outward things that believers did, but they must not have truly had Christ in their hearts.

EXPLORE

When Abraham was trying to bargain with God over the fate of those in Sodom and Gomorrah, he suggested that God would surely do what is right (see Gen. 18:25). We can trust in this truth. We can count on the fact that God will not only always favor mercy more than justice, but that he will also never get it wrong. He knows all things. He is not going to make a mistake in assessing someone's motivations or heart. Any punishment he administers will be just, and those who experience it will fully understand its justice. They will not question if God has done what is right. Our response in the meantime is to make sure that we are dressed in appropriate righteousness for that final banquet.

PRAYER

Spirit, protect me from self-deception. Clothe me in righteousness that I may celebrate with you in the final banquet.

You were taught, with regard to your former way of life, to put off your old self, which is being corrupted by its deceitful desires; to be made new in the attitude of your minds; and to put on the new self, created to be like God in true righteousness and holiness.

—EPHESIANS 4:22–24

BRIDGING JESUS' WORLD AND OURS

In several parables, the first part has little to do with us today, because it was about the religious leaders of ancient Israel. They were the first invitees to the final banquet, and most of them refused the invitation. However, even by the time the gospels of Matthew and Luke were written, these leaders were already judged. There is no room for Christians to use these sorts of verses to justify the persecution of Jews.

More important is that we respond to God's invitation and that we dress appropriately. In the parable of the great banquet in Luke, some make excuses that really show that they are not willing to make the king their first priority. They are not true followers of Christ, only halfhearted ones.

Still others do not dress appropriately for the banquet. Matthew 22 goes on to say what God expects us to wear in his kingdom: love. We are to love him by submitting entirely to his will, and we are to love our neighbors and enemies as ourselves. That is the dress code for the kingdom.

EXERCISE

Reflect on all that you have done this week. Can you discern any moments when the King invited you to participate in his kingdom? Did you answer the call or make excuses? Celebrate or repent as necessary.

PARABLES OF THE END
Matthew 25

Come, you who are blessed by my Father;
take your inheritance, the kingdom prepared
for you since the creation of the world.

—MATTHEW 25:34

Day 1

BE READY
Matthew 25:1–13

INTRODUCTION

Matthew 25 has three parables that all have to do with the final judgment. The first is the parable of the ten virgins. Some of these virgins are ready when the bridegroom comes, but some are not and end up being unable to participate in the wedding banquet.

ENGAGE

In the parable of the ten virgins, all ten are waiting for the bridegroom to come, perhaps to be part of the wedding procession and festivities. One translation calls them "bridesmaids" (NRSV). However, the bridegroom does not come as quickly as they had expected. All of the bridesmaids fall asleep waiting, their lamps continuing to burn all the while. When the bridegroom finally comes at midnight, five of them still have enough oil to go with him. The other five, who did not anticipate how long they were going to have to wait, do not have enough oil for the procession. By the time they get more, it is too late. They miss the wedding and the festivities.

Give me oil in my lamp, keep me burning.
Give me oil in my lamp, I pray. . . .
Keep me burning till the break of day.

—A. SEVISON

EXAMINE

This parable, like so many of the parables and teachings in Matthew, warns that not everyone who seems to follow Jesus will be part of the kingdom when it finally comes. We saw this shocking theme in the parable of the weeds. We see it in Matthew 7:21–23 when Jesus says not everyone who cries, "Lord, Lord," will be part of the kingdom, even though they have prophesied and cast out demons. We will see it again in the parable of the sheep and goats. In the parable of the ten virgins, some of those who start out waiting for Jesus' return do not make it, because they have run out of "spiritual juice." They are not ready, and the Lord denies that he knows them.

EXPLORE

It is doubtful that any of the New Testament authors realized at the time that the church would still be waiting for the return of the bridegroom two thousand years later. Yet amazingly, this parable about the delay of the bridegroom anticipates that Jesus may be some time in returning. How can we keep our lamps burning? How can we prepare by keeping enough oil for our lamps? It is about our love not growing cold before the end (24:12). It is about continuing to be faithful. From the verses immediately preceding (24:45–51), it is about serving God's people fairly and using God's possessions in service of others. It is about doing the master's business, as the parable that immediately follows will indicate.

PRAYER

Spirit, keep my lamp filled with your oil. May my love for God and others never grow cold.

Day 2

KEEP BUSY
Matthew 25:14–23

INTRODUCTION

Today we look at the first half of the parable of the bags of gold, often called the parable of the talents. Like the parable of the ten virgins, it is about how we pass the time while waiting for the Lord to return.

ENGAGE

The beginning of this parable suggests that the parable of the talents has a similar meaning to the parable of the ten virgins. The master is away and will not be returning for a time. Like the virgins, we need to be ready for his return. In this parable, being ready means using the master's resources in a way that multiplies and grows them. The first two servants are rewarded when the master returns, because they have been diligent in investing the master's money. Like most interpreters over the centuries, I suspect that the parable is about more than money. Like the parable that follows, we increase the master's resources by doing good in the world, bringing fruits of righteousness.

EXAMINE

The parable of the talents sounds so much like contemporary, capitalistic values that it would be easy to throw out all of Jesus' teaching on money elsewhere and focus on this parable alone. "See," the interpretation might go, "making money is a good thing, and God hates the person who is lazy with money and doesn't work hard to earn a living." The key, though, is what the money or resources are being used for. The point of the parable is not that they are for personal pleasure or luxury. In fact, they are not our resources at all. We are using God's resources for the benefit of his purposes. The parable that follows makes it clear that "investing" the master's resources significantly includes using them to help others in need.

EXPLORE

We should probably read this parable in terms of using all the gifts and opportunities God has given us to do good in the world. For some of us, God has given us wealth and great material resources. We should use it for the Lord. To some of us, God has given talents of intellect, musical skills, or social skills. In fact, the English word *talent* comes from this parable. In Jesus' day, a talent was an outrageous sum of money, maybe even half of an average person's life income. But Christians throughout the centuries have wisely applied the parable in terms of using the gifts God has given us to work to bring about God's will in the world until Christ comes again.

Do all the good you can. By all the means
you can. In all the ways you can. In all the places
you can. At all the times you can. To all the
people you can. As long as ever you can.

—JOHN WESLEY

PRAYER

Father, give me the courage to use the gifts and opportunities you have given me, expecting you to perform miracles in the world through me.

Day 3

NO FEAR
Matthew 25:24–30

INTRODUCTION

Today we look at the second half of the parable of the talents. Strict judgment is doled out to the servant who did not use the resources the master gave him, but instead buried them in the ground.

ENGAGE

After the master rewards the two servants who doubled their money, he finds out that the third servant buried his money in the ground. This servant was afraid to use the resources the master gave him. The master throws him "outside, into the darkness, where there [is] weeping and gnashing of teeth" (25:30). The master utters harsh words—whoever does not have will lose even what he or she has. Ultimately, the meaning is surely about having faith and the confidence to live for the good news. God will entrust the person who has this faith, this commitment to God's mission, with more and more to do for the kingdom. The one without faith will not make it into the kingdom.

Always be prepared to give an answer
to everyone who asks you to give the reason
for the hope that you have.

—1 PETER 3:15

EXAMINE

If those who invest the master's money are those who occupy themselves using the resources the master has given them in order to do good, then the one who buries the bag of gold in the ground is someone who shrinks back in fear. This person does not spread the good news. Such people do not use the gifts God has given them. We remember sayings of Jesus like Matthew 10:32–33: "Whoever acknowledges me before others, I will also acknowledge before my Father in heaven. But whoever disowns me before others, I will disown before my Father in heaven." Such people put their hands to the plow and then turn back (see Luke 9:62). This person plays it safe in the world and accomplishes little for God.

EXPLORE

We can certainly apply this parable to the individual who does not use the gifts and resources God has given him or her. But perhaps even more, this parable reminds us that serving the Lord means going all-in. Serving the king is not something you do halfheartedly. If we are not willing to confess Christ before the world, the Lord will not confess us as his in the judgment. If we do not have the courage to use the resources God has given us for others or in service of the gospel, we will not be welcome into the kingdom. "The Spirit God gave us does not make us timid, but gives us power, love and self-discipline" (2 Tim. 1:7).

PRAYER

Spirit, give me the courage to confess you before the world, even when it is not easy or convenient.

Day 4

DON'T BE A GOAT
Matthew 25:31–33, 41–46

INTRODUCTION

The final "end times" parable in Matthew is the parable of the sheep and the goats. In this parable, the Son of Man (Jesus) brings all the nations before his throne and separates the good (sheep) from the bad (goats) for the final judgment.

ENGAGE

The goats in this parable are told to depart from Jesus into eternal fire, a fire God arguably did not create for humanity initially, but for the Devil and his fallen angels (25:41). The reason for their demise is the fact that they had not fed Jesus when he was hungry, had not given him something to drink when he was thirsty. They had not invited him into their houses when Jesus came to town as a visitor, an immigrant. They did not clothe him when they saw Jesus naked. They did not visit him when he was in prison. Of course, Jesus was not really referring to himself. He was referring to people in need whom they could have helped but did not.

EXAMINE

This parable is a fitting climax to the theme we have seen in so many of Matthew's parables that some individuals will be taken by surprise at the judgment because they think they are "in" when in fact they are not. Not all historical Pharisees were legalists, but the idea of a Pharisee is a fitting image of what religious people can so easily become. We assume we are in because we go to church and do respectable, religious things. Maybe we are born into a Christian family. But our hearts can stray. In the words of Matthew 15:8, "These people honor me with their lips, but their hearts are far from me." The proof is in the pudding, as the saying goes. Do you live out God's love?

EXPLORE

The parable mentions how those with resources did not help brothers or sisters in need. For Jesus, such brothers would have been any fellow Israelite, whether a follower of him or not. Today, someone might want to wiggle out of the point by arguing that Christians are only obligated to take care of fellow Christians, not just anyone in need. But if you look at Jesus' teaching about loving not just friends but enemies, it seems quite certain that Jesus believed we have a Christian responsibility to *anyone* in need. As he said, "If you love those who love you, what reward will you get? Are not even the tax collectors doing that?" (Matt. 5:46). Jesus' warning here has to do with how we treat *anyone* in such circumstances.

Faith by itself, if it is not accompanied by action,
is dead. . . . Show me your faith without deeds,
and I will show you my faith by my deeds.
You believe that there is one God. Good! Even
the demons believe that—and shudder.

—James 2:17–19

PRAYER

Spirit, purge me of a spirit looking for excuses not to do God's will. Give me a bold spirit to do more than you ask.

Day 5

BE A SHEEP
Matthew 25:34–40

INTRODUCTION

Obviously we want to be sheep rather than goats. The sheep have been doing things with the heart of Christ without even seeming to realize it. They seem surprised to be rewarded for doing what was in their hearts to do.

ENGAGE

At the judgment, the Son of Man invites the sheep into his eternal kingdom. These sheep gave Jesus food when he was hungry and drink when he was thirsty. They invited him in when he had nowhere to stay and clothes when he was naked. They looked after him when he was sick and brought him food in prison. The sheep did not realize they had done these things. Jesus reveals that when they did it to brothers and sisters in need, they were in effect helping him. Since Jesus was addressing the nations, Jesus may have been calling the poor everywhere his family, even if they were not believers. These righteous individuals, who helped, have eternal life.

Nobody cares how much you know, until
they know how much you care.

—THEODORE ROOSEVELT

EXAMINE

In this scene, God judges all the nations of the world. It is interesting that Jesus' criteria for eternal reward here is not faith in him. The idea of "justification by faith" is not mentioned in this story. And Jesus is not just talking to believers either, who we could say already had faith. The only criteria for salvation that Jesus mentioned in this parable is good works toward those in need. Those of us who are Protestants are so indoctrinated in justification by faith alone that we should pause for a minute to balance out our theology. The role of loving works of mercy is so central to our eternal destiny that Jesus can tell a story where it is the *only* criteria mentioned.

EXPLORE

For the better part of the twentieth century, a segment of American Christianity ironically considered the acts of mercy celebrated in this parable as "liberal" and therefore unchristian. Although many have come around in the last few decades to accept that it is at least OK to minister to the needy, such ministries can still bear a stigma. For example, some Christians pit evangelism against helping the needy. They might say that it is fine to help the needy as long as it does not distract from the mission of the church or take away resources for evangelism. This parable does not agree. To Jesus, helping those in need is every bit as much a part of the mission as leading others to repentance.

PRAYER

Jesus, give me a heart to help those I can, and may I do it because I want to do it, not because I have to.

BRIDGING JESUS' WORLD AND OURS

Most people either like the idea of God's judgment too much or too little. Those who like it too much may be too keen to see others condemned to hell. Those who like it too little may not like the idea of God holding people accountable for the way they have lived.

Whether we like it or not, hell is part of the New Testament. And while we may not associate hell with Jesus' teaching, the book of Matthew has more imagery of hell-fire than any other part of the Bible. It is not, however, something that should preoccupy those who trust in Christ. God apparently did not create eternal fire for humanity, although many unfortunately will experience it. We know that however God administrates our eternal destinies, he will do what is just.

What we should be focusing on instead is being ready and occupying ourselves with righteousness until he returns. The parables this week highlight the responsibilities we have to love those in need and to use the resources God has given us for good. May we all serve God in the world so naturally that we are surprised to be rewarded for it!

EXERCISE

Picture yourself today standing before Jesus' glorious throne on the day of judgment. Jesus is about to separate the sheep from the goats. Ask him in prayer today which side you are headed for. Adjust your life as necessary.